The Life of

J.L. Kraft

The man who changed cheese

Rebecca Vickers

Heinemann
LIBRARY

www.heinemann.co.uk/library
Visit our website to find out more information about **Heinemann Library** books.

To order:
Phone 44 (0) 1865 888066
Send a fax to 44 (0) 1865 314091
Visit the Heinemann Bookshop at www.heinemann.co.uk/library to browse our catalogue and order online.

First published in Great Britain by Heinemann Library, Halley Court, Jordan Hill, Oxford OX2 8EJ, part of Harcourt Education.
Heinemann is a registered trademark of Harcourt Education Ltd.

Editorial: Traci Todd and Harriet Milles
Design: Richard Parker and Maverick Design
Picture Research: Julie Laffin
Production: Camilla Smith

Originated by Repro Multi-Warna
Printed and bound in China by
South China Printing Company

The paper used to print this book comes from sustainable resources.

ISBN 0 431 18100 4 (hardback)
09 08 07 06 05
10 9 8 7 6 5 4 3 2 1

ISBN 0 431 18159 4 (paperback)
10 09 08 07 06
10 9 8 7 6 5 4 3 2 1

British Library Cataloguing in Publication Data
Rebecca Vickers
J. L. Kraft – (The Life of)
338. 7'664'0092
A full catalogue record for this book is available from the British Library.

Acknowledgements
The Publishers would like to thank the following for permission to reproduce photographs:
p. **4** Image Bank Film/Getty Images; pp. **5, 7, 13, 14, 18, 19, 20, 21, 22, 23, 25, 26** Kraft Foods Inc.; p. **6, 17** The Granger Collection; pp. **8, 9, 10, 11, 12, 16** Corbis; p. **8** North Wind Picture Archives; p. **15** W.K. Kellogg Foundation; p. **24** Andrew E. Cook; p. **27** David McNew/Getty Images

Cover photograph by Kraft Foods Inc.
Cover and interior icons Janet Lankford Moran/Heinemann Library

Disclaimer
All the Internet addresses (URLs) given in this book were valid at the time of going to press. However, due to the dynamic nature of the Internet, some addresses may have changed, or sites may have changed or ceased to exist since publication. While the author and Publishers regret any inconvenience this may cause readers, no responsibility for any such changes can be accepted by either the author or the Publishers.

Contents

Words shown in the text in bold, **like this**, are explained in the Glossary.

From fresh to processed

Fresh food is good for you. Putting food in the fridge keeps some of it fresh, but after a time **bacteria** grows. This can make food go bad.

Fresh cheese is very tasty, but it can easily go bad.

James Lewis Kraft wanted to make food last longer before going bad. He built up a big **business**, making **processed** cheese and other foods.

J.L. Kraft **invented** a way to make food last longer.

The early years

James Lewis Kraft (called J.L.) was born on 11 November 1874, near Lake Erie in Ontario, Canada. His parents were George and Minerva Kraft.

These are early photographs of J.L.'s parents.

The home where J.L. grew up would have looked like this one.

J.L. had ten brothers and sisters. He was the second oldest child. His father was a farmer.

Working hard

J.L.'s family was very religious. They believed in the Bible and lived very simple lives.

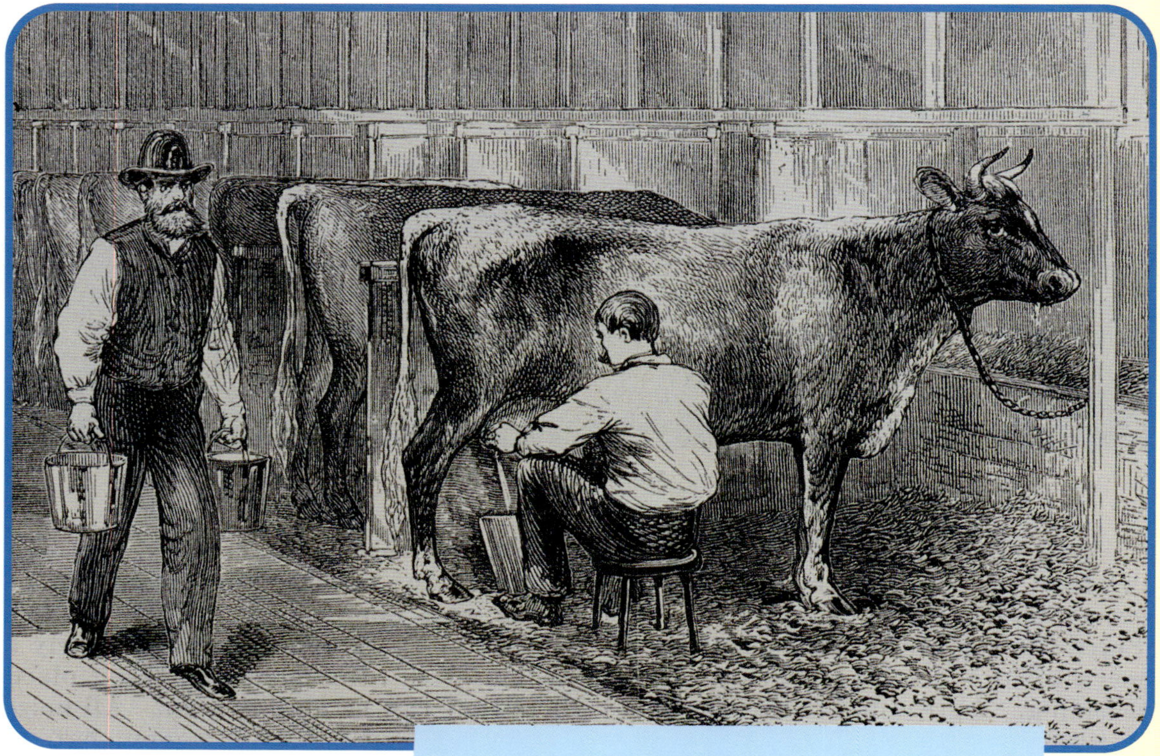

J.L. and his family lived and worked on a farm like this one.

In most small towns, the **general store** was the only place to buy things.

J.L. went to the local school and worked hard to help his father on the farm. His first job was at Ferguson's general store in Fort Erie, Ontario, Canada.

Crossing the border

J.L. worked at Ferguson's for about ten years. In 1902, he moved from Canada to the USA. He became a **partner** in a cheese **company** in Buffalo, New York.

Buffalo was much bigger than the small town in Canada where J.L. had been living.

J.L. left Buffalo to work for the company in Chicago, Illinois. Sadly for J.L., his partners turned against him. He ended up with no job and only 65 US dollars!

In the early 1900s, Chicago was the second-largest city in the USA.

Trading in cheese

In Chicago, J.L. started to buy and sell cheese. He bought cheese early in the morning from a **market**. He then sold it to grocery shops.

Grocery shop owners liked buying from J.L. It meant they did not have to get up early to go to a market like this one.

J.L. first sold his cheese to grocery shops from a horse-drawn cart.

In 1909, J.L. started the J.L. Kraft and Brothers **Company**. Four of J.L.'s brothers came to work for him. By 1914, the company sold 30 kinds of cheese across the USA.

A wife and a daughter

In 1910, J.L. married Pauline Elizabeth Platt. In 1916, J.L. and Pauline had a daughter, who they called Edith.

This picture shows J.L. and Pauline with their daughter, Edith.

At the same time, W.K. Kellogg, the cereal maker (seen here), also tried to keep foods fresh.

Soon after his marriage, J.L. became an American **citizen**. He was also working hard to find a way to keep cheese from going bad.

Cheese goes to war

In 1914, **World War I** started in Europe. The USA joined the war in 1917. American soldiers needed food **rations**.

More than 2 million American soldiers came to Europe to fight in World War I.

The US **government** bought huge amounts of Kraft's tinned cheese during World War I.

J.L. had worked out a way to **process** cheese to keep it fresh. The US Army decided to include tins of Kraft processed cheese in the soldiers' rations.

Processing and patents

J.L.'s **company** made **processed** cheese that lasted a long time. Over the years, Kraft and Brothers took out many **patents** so that no one could steal their ideas.

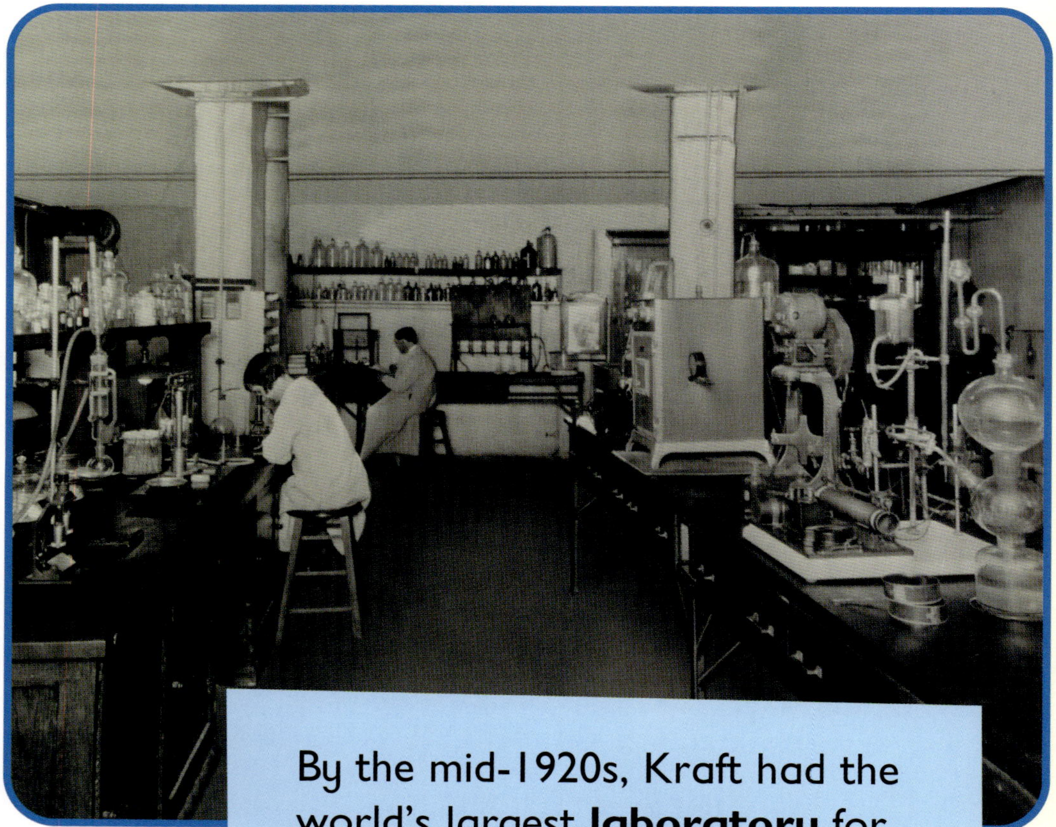

By the mid-1920s, Kraft had the world's largest **laboratory** for working on cheese.

Another company, Phenix Cheese, also made processed cheese. In 1928, the two companies joined to become the Kraft-Phenix Cheese Corporation.

The Phenix Cheese Company was famous for its *Philadelphia Cream Cheese*.

Advertising and entertainment

J.L. Kraft believed in **advertising**. To begin with, he used local newspapers. When the **company** got bigger, it advertised in popular magazines.

Kraft products were advertised to show how they could be used.

Kraft Television Theatre was shown on American television from 1947 to 1958.

In the 1930s, Kraft **sponsored** an American radio programme called *Kraft Music Hall*. Later, the company sponsored the first big television drama programme, *Kraft Television Theatre*.

Kraft Foods

The Kraft-Phenix Cheese Corporation grew quickly. By the early 1930s, it had 10,000 workers in the USA and four other countries.

By the 1940s, Kraft was making much more than cheese. It changed its name to Kraft Foods.

In 1928, *Velveeta* was **invented**. This is one of the most popular Kraft products. *Miracle Whip* and *Kraft Macaroni and Cheese Dinner* went on sale in the 1930s.

Kraft Macaroni and Cheese Dinner is still one of Kraft's most popular products.

After the war

By 1945, J.L. Kraft was a very successful man. He still made time for his hobby, collecting a green stone called **jade**. He collected jade from all over the world.

J.L. Kraft made this window from jade. It is in a church in Chicago.

J.L. stopped working for Kraft Foods in 1951. He died in Chicago on 16 February 1953, when he was 78 years old.

This is a photograph of J.L. in his later years.

More about J.L.

J.L. Kraft was not just successful at **inventing** and **business**. He was also good to his workers, and he gave away a lot of his money.

J.L. and Pauline worked together to make life better for other people.

Today, Kraft Foods products are made and sold all around the world. There are Kraft Foods offices and factories in more than 150 countries.

As well as cheese, Kraft Foods now sells coffee, chocolate, cereal, biscuits, and many other foods.

Fact file

- J.L.'s parents spelt their name 'Krafft'. J.L. changed it so that it was spelt with just one 'f'.
- J.L. was an expert on the valuable stone, **jade**. His book on jade was published in 1947.
- One of the most popular foods in Australia is the spread *Vegemite*. It is made by Kraft.
- Kraft Foods still sells more cheese than any other **company** in the world.

Timeline

1874	James L. Kraft is born in Canada on 11 November
1902	J.L. leaves Canada for the USA
1903	J.L. moves to Chicago, Illinois
1909	J.L. Kraft and Brothers Company is set up
1910	J.L. marries Pauline Elizabeth Platt
1911	J.L. becomes an American **citizen**
1916	J.L. Kraft and Brothers takes out first **patents** on cheese **processing**
1919	The first colour **advertising** of Kraft products in popular magazines
1928	Kraft Cheese Company and Phenix Cheese Company become the Kraft-Phenix Cheese Corporation
1945	The company name becomes Kraft Foods Company
1951	J.L. hands over job as head of Kraft Foods to his younger brother, John
1953	James L. Kraft dies on 16 February

Glossary

advertise show or tell people about something they can buy

bacteria very small living things

business activity that earns money

citizen official member of a country

company group of people who makes money by selling things

general store shop that sells everything

government group that leads the country and makes laws

invent make something that has never been made before

jade hard green stone

laboratory place where scientific work is done

market where people buy or sell things

partners owners of a company

patent ownership of an idea or invention to so no one can copy it

processing method used to change something

rations packages of food for soldiers

sponsored paid to advertise

World War I war fought in Europe from 1914 to 1918

Find out more

Books

Cheese, Claire Kreger (Blackbirch Press, 2003)

Websites

www.kraftfoods.co.uk

Kraft's own website will give you information about the company and their products.

Index